For Dear K

CU00823121

NORTH JERSEY
THROUGH TIME
Keith E. Morgan

With Love and Best Wishes,

Keith E Morgan

x x

1st. July 2013

AMBERLEY PUBLISHING

Where shall we visit next? This sign post used to stand in front of the Café Capri on The Green at Gorey in June 1960.

This book is dedicated to Malvina, 'My Special Angell',
in memory of all the great holidays that we had together on the island of Jersey.

First published 2013

Amberley Publishing
The Hill, Stroud, Gloucestershire, GL5 4EP
www.amberley-books.com

Copyright © Keith E. Morgan, 2013

The right of Keith E. Morgan to be identified as the Author of this work has been asserted in accordance with the Copyrights, Designs and Patents Act 1988.

ISBN 978 1 4456 1401 4 (print)
ISBN 978 1 4456 1416 8 (ebook)

All rights reserved. No part of this book may be reprinted or reproduced or utilised in any form or by any electronic, mechanical or other means, now known or hereafter invented, including photocopying and recording, or in any information storage or retrieval system, without the permission in writing from the Publishers.

British Library Cataloguing in Publication Data.
A catalogue record for this book is available from the British Library.

Typesetting by Amberley Publishing.
Printed in Great Britain.

Introduction

This is the third publication in the Jersey *Through Time* series that traces the island's history through the medium of photography. What was initially to be a single volume has developed into a series, in order to incorporate and do justice to the very many photographs that have been acquired by the author for the project.

Covering the north and hinterland of Jersey, this book starts at Gorey where the previous book, entitled *South Jersey Through Time*, finished. From Gorey, the reader is guided around the north coast of the island, taking in the picturesque little bays and inlets, diverting where necessary to take in areas of the hinterland that had not been covered by the previous two books, before reaching Jersey Airport in the west. The latter was the starting point for *South Jersey Through Time*, so between them the two publications have completely circumnavigated the island, not by sea, but by land in an anti-clockwise direction.

The north coast of the island is quite distinct from that of the south, being more rugged and steep, with windy roads that have sharp hairpin bends leading down to the picturesque little bays and harbours. There are not so many defensive structures along the northern coastline as it was felt that the steep cliffs themselves provided a sufficient and formidable natural deterrent against attack from the sea.

The opportunity has been taken to include the States of Jersey Police and the Pallot Steam, Motor & General Museum in this publication. The States of Jersey Police celebrated its 60th anniversary in 2012. The organisation has a vast collection of historical photographs in its archive to which complete freedom of access was given to the author for use in both the current book and any future publications. Similarly the Pallot Steam, Motor & General Museum also has a vast archive of photographs and records, to which the author was given free access. In addition, the museum has a magnificent collection of both static and working exhibits that also provided a good subject source for photographing by the author. Twice each year, the Pallot Museum brings Jersey's agricultural past to life with two magnificent steam fayres.

Finally, the reader is brought to Jersey Airport. It it here that most visitors to Jersey both start and end their visit. I trust that everyone who acquires a copy of this book will enjoy reading it as much as I have enjoyed producing it.

Keith E. Morgan

The Jersey Revels, 1204–2004
Seigneur de Carteret's entourage make their way to Gorey for the Jersey 1204–2004 Revels Celebrations in June 2004. As part of the 800th anniversary celebrations held on the island, the Revels were the biggest event of its kind ever to take place in Jersey. Below, staff at the Old Court House Hotel, Gorey, by caricature artist Edward Blampied.

Gorey Castle Then and Now
Views looking across the harbour to Mont Orgueil Castle, probably one of the most photographed locations in Jersey. Other than the type of ships in the harbour and the German fortifications on the castle, very little appears to have changed in the just over one hundred years separating the two views (top pre 1910; bottom June 2012).

Policing in Gorey

A then and now of the cars and uniforms of the States of Jersey Police. The top view is of police sergeant Tom Skinner and police constable E. Lewis dressed in their summer uniforms with their Jaguar police car at Gorey during the summer months of the 1960s. By contrast, at the same location in June 2012, police constable Chris Ingham is seen in regulation kit alongside a modern all-singing, all-dancing Skoda police car.

Gorey Village Restaurant
Contrasting views from June 1960 and June 2012. At the latter date decorations were in vogue for the football World Cup and the Queen's Diamond Jubilee.

Romance at Gorey Castle
Honeymooner Malvina Morgan enjoying the sun and view from Gorey Castle in June 1960, while local newly-weds Simon and Aneka (*née* Orr) Howard had just tied the knot at a wedding ceremony held in the castle on 6 July 2012.

The Castle Green
What was the Café Capri in June 1960 is in August 2012 the Castle Green 'gastropub', run by the Jersey Potteries.

Anne Port

The top postcard is probably of 1930s vintage, with a view of Anne Port Bay from Geoffrey's Leap, while the modern comparison view from roughly the same vantage point was taken by photographer Lauren Richards in June 2012.

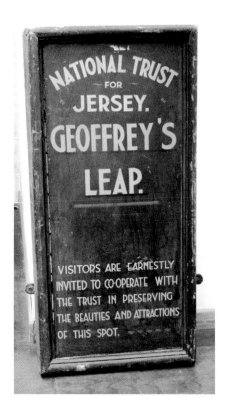

Geoffrey's Leap

The original wooden noticeboard from Geoffrey's Leap, placed there by the National Trust for Jersey (formed in 1937), is now preserved in the Pallot Steam, Motor & General Museum at Trinity. It has been replaced on the headland by a carved stone identifying the location in *Jersiaise* French as 'Le Saut Geffroy'. This is the reputed spot where Geoffrey jumped to his death, though no one really knows who Geoffrey was.

Geoffrey's Leap Café

A popular venue and landmark in the heyday of the Jersey tourism industry, the Geoffrey's Leap Café finally closed its doors in 2001 after enjoying thirty years as a tea room. Its owner passed away in 2011 and the premises was placed on the market for sale in 2012. With a marvellous view overlooking Anne Port Bay, it had not been sold when the bottom photograph was taken in July 2012.

Anne Port

Another comparison view looking along the swing of Anne Port Bay from the roadside, taken by photographer Lauren Richards in June 2012. Geoffrey's Leap Café can be readily picked out – the white building as the road curves to the left before traversing the headland.

Archirondel

Carrying on round the coast towards St Catherine's Bay, the traveller comes to the small cove of Archirondel, with its distinctive tower. The top view is again probably from the 1930s, and little seems to have changed since the scene was recaptured by photographer Lauren Richards as she journeyed around the east coast of Jersey in June 2012.

Archirondel Tower

Lauren has again taken a photograph that could be considered to have been frozen in time, as very little change appears to have taken place between the 1930s and 2012. The Archirondel Tower, also known as the Red Tower, was completed in 1794. It was constructed with a permanent masonry gun platform around its base and was the twenty-second tower to be built as part of a defensive coastal network for Jersey.

St Catherine's Bay

A natural sweeping bay, St Catherine's was chosen as a projected 'refuge' harbour for the Royal Navy fleet during the period of the Anglo-French rivalry in the 1840s. The white Martello tower of St Catherine's, like its partner at Archirondel, also serves as a navigational marker for shipping.

ST. CATHERINE'S, JERSEY.

St Catherine's Bay

The view in the top postcard shows not only the White Tower, but also the breakwater that protects the north end of the bay. Work began on the north breakwater in 1847. It was finished in 1855, by which time Britain and France were fighting as allies against the Russians. Work was started on the southern breakwater, but never completed. The hamlet of St Catherine has developed around the White Tower with the building of new houses and the RNLI lifeboat station.

Telephone Kiosks

These photographs illustrate the old telephone kiosk, in traditional wood with slated roof (late 1980s), and the modern plastic-coated metal one that replaced it at St Catherine's breakwater (June 2012).

Rozel Bay

The north coast of Jersey is much more rugged than that of the south, requiring a visitor to descend down steep and often narrow roads to access the small bays, such as Rozel Bay, along this stretch of coastline. The top postcard view was probably taken in the 1930s and shows the Rozel Bay Hotel and the once famous tropical gardens of Chateau La Claire. These gardens were designed and laid out by Samuel Curtis from 1841 until his death in 1860. The hotel still exits in 2012 as the Rozel, as do the gardens, but alas, they are now much overgrown.

Rozel Bay, Le Couperon Barracks

The barracks, which were built in 1809 to accommodate sixty-eight soldiers when the threat of a French attack was still very real, are shown in the top view, probably taken in the early 1900s. They eventually fell into disuse and dereliction, before being converted into the Le Couperon de Rozel Hotel. In turn, the establishment became the Beau Couperon Hotel, but by 2012 it had again fallen into disuse and renovation work appeared to be at a standstill. The bottom picture shows the hotel in June 1994, while it was still a commercial concern.

Rozel Bay Car Parking

The bottom picture, courtesy of the *Jersey Evening Post*, was taken in June 1972 and shows that parking problems at Rozel are nothing new. With the tourist season in full swing, drivers took the law into their own hands and parked illegally on the beach, resulting in some cars getting bogged down. The top picture on the Rozel slipway is a composition of photographs taken of the author in 2012 and his wife Malvina in 1960.

ROZEL BAY, JERSEY, C.I.

Rozel Harbour

Two comparison views of Rozel Harbour. The top one was possibly taken not long after the end of the German occupation, while the lower photograph was taken in June 2012.

The Hungry Man Café.
This well-known café was established in 1947. The 1967 photograph of The Hungry Man (*top*) was provided by Barbara Wilding, whose parents once owned and ran the café. It is still going strong today, as shown in the picture taken in July 2012, with, from left to right, Marion, Katie and Terry posing in front.

Artist at Work

The Hungry Man café and quayside have been decorated by local artist Edward Blampied (*inset*). A selection of Edward's caricature-style paintings at Rozel is illustrated. These resemble the saucy postcards made famous by Donald McGill between 1904 and 1962, when he is thought to have produced 12,000 designs! Edward, you have got a long way to go to catch up!

La Tourelle

Situated on La Route des Côtes du Nord, which follows the north coast out of Rozel Bay, in 2002 La Tourelle was an exclusive hotel and restaurant. Like many other Jersey hotels it has now been converted and extended into equally exclusive apartments, as can be seen in the 2012 photograph.

The Water's Edge Hotel, Bouley Bay

Another prestigious hotel, The Water's Edge at Bouley Bay, closed its doors for holiday accommodation at the end of the 2012 tourist season – yet another sign of the changing fortunes of the tourist trade in Jersey. The hotel, like many others on the island, is being converted into apartments. Small visitor souvenir shops fronting the hotel, like the Little Anchor shown in the inset, will probably have to move on.

Bouley Bay

Another of Jersey's picturesque bays on its north coast. The road zigzags all the way down to the harbour and has become famous for hill-climb rallies and speed tests. In the summer months it was impossible for the author to replicate the scene shown in the old photograph due to the coverage given by the mature tree growth. Fortunately, professional photographer Alexis Militis stepped into the breach and saved the day by taking a shot during the month of February, when the tree foliage had died back. For all its hairpin bends, buses nevertheless manage to navigate their way successfully to and from Bouley Bay, as shown in the inset.

Bouley Bay Hill Climb

Organised by the Jersey Motor Cycle & Light Car Club, the first Bouley Bay Hill Climb was held in 1920. Today, the club organises four hill climbs a year. The hill climb stopped briefly during the German occupation of the island, but started again in 1946 with an international event. The following year, Bouley Bay was one of only five venues in the inaugural British Hill Climb Championship and has held championship events every since. The top picture, courtesy of the *Jersey Evening Post*, shows Lyndon Pallot competing in his Swallow Doretti in the Whit Monday 1958 Hill Climb Championship, while photographer Lauren Richards has captured a scene from a 2012 hill climb.

Bouley Bay Hill Climb

Past hill-climb champion Lyndon Pallot is shown waiting for the 'off' in the June 1957 Hill Climb Championship (picture courtesy of the *Jersey Evening Post*), while racing driver Jos Goodyear in his GWR Raptor Extreme 1598cc is captured breaking the course hill-climb record by photographer Lauren Richards in the July 2012 British Hill Climb Championship below. Jos lowered the outright hill-climb record at Bouley Bay to an incredible 37.82 seconds. Originally 1,065 yards in length, the overall distance of the hill climb was reduced to the current 1,011 yards in 1949.

The Durell Wildlife Conservation Trust

The late Gerald Durrell established the Jersey Zoo in 1959 at Les Augres Manor as a sanctuary and breeding centre for endangered species. Subsequently, in 1963 Durell changed the name and founded the Jersey Wildlife Preservation Trust as a charitable institution. Durell died in January 1995 and the trust was renamed the Durell Wildlife Conservation Trust in its founder's honour on 26 March 1999. The trust is a conservation organisation with a mission to save species from extinction, hence the use of the well-known extinct dodo bird as its symbol. The photographs illustrate the dodo atop the entrance pillars as well as in the inset. Durrell himself has also been immortalised in a statue erected within the trust grounds.

St Martin's Church

Two very contrasting views of St Martin's church. The first was probably taken before the First World War, as the war memorial has yet to be erected, while the second photograph was taken on 6 July 2010 and shows how the church is now bereft of the trees that once surrounded it.

La Hougue Bie

La Hougue Bie is a Neolithic site. The chapel was built on the top of the mound in the twelfth century, and its ruins were subsequently transformed into an aristocratic home in the neo-Gothic style shortly after 1780 by the D'Auvergne family. The latter home had a castellated wall and two impressive towers, as shown in the old photograph, which is date-stamped July 1916. It was known as the Prince's Tower because Phillippe D'Auvergne was heir to the Prince de Boullion. After a period of decay, the Prince's Tower Hotel was constructed on the site during the 1830s, only to close its doors in the early 1920s, with the Prince's Tower being demolished in 1924. Today, as shown in the 2012 photograph, only the reconstructed and conserved chapel remains on top of the mound.

La Hougue Bie: The Chapel of Notre Dame de la Clarté

The chapel was built in the twelfth century, possibly replacing an older wooden structure. Following use for about four centuries, the Jerusalem chapel and crypt were added in 1520 by Richard Mabon, the Dean of Jersey. The complex was abandoned around 1540, during the Protestant Reformation, and fell into ruin. The chapels were extensively rebuilt in 1925, as shown in the top print, and reconstructed in 1931, as illustrated in the lower photograph, which was taken in July 2012. The inset shows sisters Jacqueline and Malvina 'trapped' in the crypt in June 1989.

La Hougue Bie: The Passage Grave

La Hougue Bie is a Neolithic ritual site that was in use about 5,500 years ago, and is one of the largest and best-preserved passage graves in Europe. The grave itself was discovered in 1924 during excavations by the Société Jersiaise, who had recently bought the site. The structure consists of a narrow, 9.6m-long passage leading into a large oval chamber, 9m long by 3.6m wide, with two small side chambers projecting from the north and south walls. The two photographs illustrate the excavation work carried out on the grave entrance in June 1994 and the end result as seen in July 2012.

La Rue à Don Well

This well, or *lavoir*, is just a short distance from Longueville Manor and situated on a rather sharp bend of La Rue à Don. In the June 1961 picture, newly-wed Jacqueline Bate is sampling the pure water that pours continuously from the well. If it was used for communal washing in the past, it would have been called a *douet à laver*, as they are known to Jersey country people, or a *lavoir*. Pure water still flows continuously from the well, as illustrated in the photograph taken by the author on 11 August 2010.

St Saviour's Church

Unlike St Martin's church on page 31, trees have been allowed to grow around the church, obscuring the view of the building, as seen in the photograph taken in June 2012. The church is famous because it was the benefice of the Dean of Jersey. One of the holders of this office was the father of Lillie Langtry, the famous daughter of Jersey known throughout the world as the 'Jersey Lily'. Born in 1853 as Emilie Charlotte Le Breton, Lillie died in Monaco in 1929 aged seventy-five. Her body was brought back to Jersey and her bust (shown in the inset) surmounts her grave in St Saviour's churchyard. Fame followed Lillie throughout her life, and she was the first woman to break the bank at Monte Carlo in 1907.

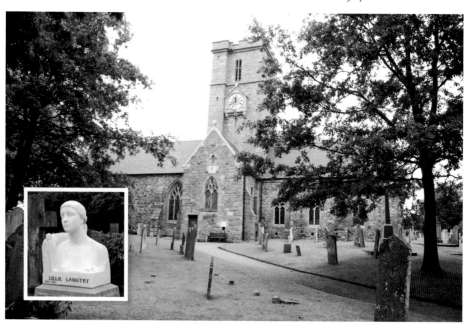

The Old Rectory, St Saviour's Church

The Old Rectory was the home of the Le Breton family and the birthplace in 1853 of Emilie Charlotte Le Breton, alias Lillie Langtry. The building has changed very little over the years, as can be seen from the two photographs. The old postcard is franked 14 January 1923, while the colour print was taken on 27 June 2012.

Government House

Government House is the official residence of the Lieutenant Governor of Jersey, currently General Sir John McColl KCB, CBE, DSO. It is also the official residence of the head of state, the Duke of Normandy – Her Majesty Queen Elizabeth II. In 1803, the rector of St Saviour's church bought the land on which the current Government House is situated and built a property there. Subsequently, the estate was bought by shipowner Francois Janvrin in 1814. He demolished the rector's house and built a two-storey property in its place. Called 'Belmont', it was acquired in 1822 by Major-General Sir Colin Halkett, the Lieutenant Governor at the time, and it has served as Government House ever since.

Government House Lodge

Two views of the lodge that guards the entrance and approach to Government House. The first photograph was probably taken during the early 1900s, judging by the uniforms worn by the sentries on duty. Except for the absence of sentries, very little has changed between then and June 2012, when the lower photograph was taken.

The States of Jersey Police: Squad Cars
Police squad cars of yesteryear (Vauxhall, 1952) and today (Mitsubishi, June 2012) with Sgt Robbie Herd and PC Chris Ingham.

The States of Jersey Police: Uniforms

Retired PC Stuart Elliott models the white summer uniform for the 50th anniversary celebrations of the States of Jersey Police in 2002. By a contrast, PC Neil Stubbs is wearing the white summer traditional-style police helmet, reintroduced in 2012.

The States of Jersey Police: Motorcycles
The States of Jersey Police have progressed via a number of different models of motorbike over the years: the ex-Second World War Corgi folding scooter was parachuted with airborne troops during the war and is being used in the 1946 photograph by PC Bert Jardine (*top left*); in the 1960s the lightweight cowled motorcycle was in use (*top right*); and by the 1980s the police had a fleet of eight motorcycles available for patrol duties (*below*).

The States of Jersey Police: Motorcycles
In 2012, the States of Jersey Police took delivery of a number of ultra-modern, powerful BMW motorbikes for patrol duties on the island. These motorbikes are being demonstrated in the photographs by police motorcycle trainer Bob Blake, right, and below, from left to right, PC Lee Scotland, Bob Blake, and PC Ian Thompson.

States of Jersey Police: Foot Patrol

Another form of transport used by the States of Jersey Police has been, and still is, the pedal bicycle, as shown in the top photograph taken in King Street, St Helier, in 1971. Bicycles have been used by the police in Jersey since the 1890s. She is not on her bike, but WPC Gemma Coles poses for a snapshot at the same location in June 2012. Gemma works on a par with her male colleagues and has a long family history in the police force, following in the footsteps of her father, Sgt Anthony Coles, and her grandfather, Sgt Harry Coles. This equality policy was endorsed early in 2013 when Insp. Alison Fossey was promoted to become Jersey's most senior female police officer, as chief inspector for crime operations.

Women Police Officers, States of Jersey Police

The first woman police cadet, Madeleine Todd, was appointed in 1963. By 1967, when the *Jersey Evening Post* took the top photograph, many women had qualified as women police constables, and the police ladies' team had secured the St John Ambulance Association First Aid Competition Philip Le Masurier Memorial Trophy, shown held by WPC Mary Staley. WP Cadet Barbara Wilding (on extreme right and inset), with forty-two years' service, went on to become one of Jersey's famous daughters as the longest serving woman chief constable in the British Isles. Today women police officers, such as those in the 2012 photograph – left to right, PC Emma Coxshall, Sgt Collette Beechey, PC Emma Dupre and Insp. Sarah Henderson – are well represented in the States of Jersey Police Force.

60th Anniversary, States of Jersey Police Through Time
In 2012, The States of Jersey Police celebrated its 60th Anniversary and issued a medallion to record the event. Chief Officer Mike Bowron QPM also took the opportunity to reintroduce the white police helmet for use in the summer months. He is standing on the left of the bottom-right photograph, with police officers wearing the new headgear alongside and in the bottom-left photograph.

Pallot Heritage Steam Museum

The museum was founded by Lyndon Charles Pallot, known as 'Don'. With an interest in mechanics from an early age, Don progressed from remaking bicycles, through engineering training on the Jersey Railway, to finally opening the Central Motor Works at Sion, Trinity, in the early 1930s. An inventor of several farm implements, it was inevitable that he was to establish the Pallot Steam Museum, which opened in 1990. Don is shown in the top photograph with one of his working steam engines, while below in 2012, alongside the same working steam engine, are members of his family, who are also the trustees of the museum, from left to right: son Lyndon, daughters Dolly and Liz, and son Sam.

Agricultural Threshing Machine, Pallot Heritage Steam Museum

The top picture shows a typical agricultural threshing machine that was once used in Jersey at harvest time throughout the early and mid-1990s. Sam Pallot has restored one of these threshing machines and is shown describing it to retired farmer Les Gilder, centre, and his wife Myra in the lower photograph. Together with a restored steam traction engine *Dolly May*, the threshing machine is put into action during one of the two annual steam fayres held at the museum each year.

Agricultural Traction Engine, Pallot Heritage Steam Museum

The museum was established with the objective of promoting the permanent preservation of steam engines, farm machinery, vehicles and much more. An excellent example of how this preservation work has been achieved is the Ransomes, Sims & Jefferies' traction engine. The engine was lying derelict at St Brelade's Bay when the young Marianne Heys chose to pose alongside it for the top photograph in the early 1960s. Since that time, the traction engine, built in Ipswich in 1904, has been restored to pristine working order, and it drives the threshing machine each year at the annual steam fayres. Named *Dolly May* in memory of Don's wife of sixty-two years, it stands gleaming in the museum, as shown in the bottom photograph, which shows Gerald Davis of Cefn Cribwr, South Wales, standing alongside in March 2012.

Albion Merryweather Fire Engine, Pallot Heritage Steam Museum
Built in 1934 at an original price of £1,500, the Albion Merryweather
fire engine entered service at St Helier in January 1935. Before being
eventually replaced after approximately twenty years, it attended all major
fires on the island, including those during the German occupation. The
top photograph, from the Denis Holmes Collection, shows the fire engine
in service just after the end of the occupation, while the bottom picture,
taken in 2011, serves to demonstrate the excellent restoration work carried
out on vehicles at the Pallot Museum. In 1978, the Albion Merryweather
fire engine successfully completed a charity round trip to Paris.

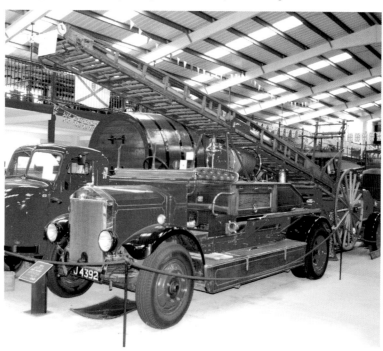

Annual Steam Fayres, Pallot Heritage Steam Museum

The Pallot Heritage Steam Museum holds two annual steam fayres every year, at which 'Jersey's past is brought back to life' in a very impressive way! At these fayres, the steam train runs regular trips around the museum's closed-circuit railway track (as it does every Thursday throughout the holiday season), while *Dolly May* the traction engine is linked to the threshing machine and drives it under full steam to thresh hay. To add to the atmosphere of the occasion, Liz Vivian *née* Pallot wears an authentic Jersey concertina bonnet (*inset*). Together with all the other exhibits on show, the steam fayres and museum are well worth a visit.

Trinity Manor

Trinity has the reputation of being one of the most rural of Jersey's twelve parishes; it is the third-largest by surface area and yet the third-smallest by population. Trinity Manor is the home of the Seigneur of Trinity, the current owner of the title being Pamela Bell, Dame of Trinity. Elaborate reconstruction of the property took place between 1910 and 1913; it was much criticised for turning the building into at French-style château. In comparing the two photographs of the front of the property, little has changed since the initial reconstruction was carried out.

Trinity Manor
Like the front of Trinity Manor, the rear also reflects the French château style and shows very little change today from the original reconstruction.

Trinity Manor Farm

Trinity Manor Farm is set in the spectacular grounds of Trinity Manor and is a highly productive and modern unit. The farm buildings were completely renovated in 1998, making way for a state-of-the-art dairy complex for 180 milking cows. The island has a tradition for Jersey cattle, as shown in the top postcard with the milkmaid at work filling the equally traditional Jersey milk can (*inset*). These cans were made from shaped pieces of tinplate soldered together. The lower photograph, taken in July 2012, captures Rob Stevenson, farm manager, and Gary Broster, estate manager, discussing grazing for the herd.

Trinity Church and AA Telephone Box
Situated on the crossroads at Trinity, the parish church of Les Croix with its distinctive white pyramidal spire is a notable landmark. Equally notable is the AA telephone box, which is also positioned on the crossroads; it is the last to survive in situ on Jersey and is still in working order.

THE WELL, TRINITY, JERSEY.

Trinity *Lavoir*

The *lavoir* shown in the postcard view is now well-hidden by undergrowth in the valley that leads from Trinity village down to Bouley Bay and was very difficult to find when the lower photograph was taken in 2012. There are at least two other *lavoirs* or wells in the village. *Douets à laver*, or *lavoirs*, were once used for fresh water, communal washing and were places for the exchange of local gossip between the washing women.

Bon Nuit Bay

Bon Nuit Bay is another of Jersey's picturesque small harbours on the north coast of the island with its winding access road. These two contrasting views of Bon Nuit Bay show the extent of development that has taken place in the bay over the years: the one photograph taken long before any housing development had taken place; the other in 2011 showing extensive use of the harbour by pleasure boats and the overlooking hillside for domestic buildings.

Wolf's Caves

Wolf's Caves are in no way connected to the canine species; they are reputed to have been named after a smuggler of the same name. They have been a very popular tourist attraction since Victorian times. In 1910 the attraction even boasted a hotel, as shown in the top photograph. This burned down during the occupation, and in 1975 a licensed café was built in its place. This was managed by May and Martin Brennan for the best part of twenty-five years before it closed in January 2001. In July 2012, only the remains of the viewing balcony were extant as the site was being developed as a private residence.

Wolf's Caves

Descending the steepest and highest cliff on Jersey's north coast today would be a daunting task for the fittest, but as shown in the early 1900s postcard, Victorian ladies used to follow the paths and boardwalks of this perilous descent down to Wolf's Caves in the wide ankle-length skirts that were *de rigueur* at that time. Today it is impossible to access Wolf's Caves; the paths and boardwalks have long become overgrown and lost, as shown in the July 2012 photograph, taken from the remains of the viewing balcony.

La Route du Nord Memorial

It is understood that La Route du Nord was constructed during the occupation by a local labour force in order to keep them employed and engaged on what was considered essential work – a ploy or scheme to prevent them being transported abroad by the Germans to work on the Continent. Originally, the memorial stone was placed centrally on the road but it is now repositioned in an adjoining car park alongside the road, as shown in the photograph taken in August 2011. The memorial stone (*inset*) records that 'this road is dedicated to the men and women of Jersey who suffered in the World War 1939–1945'.

Sion Chapel, St John

It is inevitable that travellers to St John will have noticed the huge Methodist chapel that dominates the area. As recorded above the entrance portico, Sion Methodist chapel was built in 1880 at a time of confidence and optimism. Sadly, those times are long past, and the costs of maintaining such a large building were too much for a congregation a fraction of what it once was. The last service was held in the chapel in the middle of June 2010, and it has now been taken over as a private enterprise. Even so, the building still has an aura of magnificence about it, as captured in the August 2011 photograph.

Parish Church, St John

St John is one of the northern parishes and it includes a significant part of the north coast path, with Bonne Nuit Bay as its direct link with the sea. At the heart of the parish is the church of St John in the Oaks, probably named because of the oak trees surrounding it, as shown in the two photographs. The church was dedicated to St John the Baptist, but the church emblem is the Maltese cross of the Knights of St John of Jerusalem. A unique church, inasmuch as one of the internal pillars was removed in 1831 to enable the congregation to see the preacher. The pillar now resides in the rectory garden.

To Mark, All the best — John Nettles

Jersey Goldsmiths and *Bergerac*

A family-owned business established in 1986 and having served visitors and locals alike for the past twenty-six years, the Jersey Goldsmiths closed its doors and left Lion Park in St Lawrence in January 2013. The company now appears to branching into the online business. One of the significant exhibits that has always been on display in the Jersey Goldsmiths is Jim Bergerac's 1947 Triumph 1800 Roadster TRA, registration No. 1610. The top postcard, autographed by actor John Nettles (the star of *Bergerac*) and kindly provided by Mark Lamerton, is reproduced by courtesy of Rocco Publishing and photographer Stuart Abraham. The bottom picture show excited sisters Jacqueline and Malvina (at the wheel) getting the *Bergerac* experience in the early 1990s.

Carrefour Selous, St Lawrence

The top photograph of the Carrefour Selous Hotel is rather unique in that it was taken during one of those rare occasions in the past when Jersey experienced heavy snows – very much like March 2013, when the north-easterly winds brought Arctic temperatures and snow to the island again. The hotel has now closed as can be seen from the lower photograph, taken in September 2012, and what was an antique shop alongside is now a Laura Ashley outlet.

Ye Olde Jersey House

Once called Ye Olde Jersey House, this establishment has been extended over the years and is now called The Priory Inn. The traditional Jersey stone toadstools that customers sat on outside while refreshing themselves have long since gone and been replaced with modern, more comfortable furniture, as can be seen in the lower August 2011 photograph. The latter also shows the extensions made to the far gable end of the building. The Priory Inn is the access and watering point for those wishing to visit the Devil's Hole.

Devil's Hole

Following a shipwreck in 1851, a statue of a devil adapted from the ship's figurehead was set up in the Devil's Hole. The top photograph shows visitor Malvina Morgan from Swansea in South Wales, above the Devil's Hole in June 1960 when a version of the Devil was still in residence (*inset*). Access down into the Devil's Hole today is barred due to the dangerous crumbling nature of the surrounding cliff face, and the hole must be viewed from the specially erected platform, as illustrated in the July 2010 photograph.

Devil's Hole

Two views of the Devil's Hole, spaced apart by many years. Today, the statue of the devil no longer inhabits the Devil's Hole. Rather he is positioned in the middle of a very green and murky pool just off the access footpath and not far from The Priory Inn (*inset*). He is probably here to discourage visitors from attempting to descend into the Devil's Hole in order to vandalise him.

Wishing Well at Ye Olde Jersey House
Equally as old as Ye Olde Jersey House, the wishing well is positioned close into the wall of an adjoining building. Now much overgrown and protected with the obligatory barrier to prevent the unauthorised recovery of coins from the well, it has always been a visitor attraction, and today coins are still thrown into it – and accompanying wishes made accordingly, no doubt.

Tower and Barracks, Grève de Lecq

The two views show both the defensive tower and the barracks at Grève de Lecq. The tower is the only one of Field Marshal Henry Seymor Conway's planned network of towers to be built on Jersey's north coast, the precipitous cliffs being considered sufficient to provide a natural defence. It was one of the first to be built in the late 1770s and unusually stands some 100 metres inland. Today, the tower serves as a navigation aid, being painted white. Designed to garrison troops, the barracks were built almost 200 years ago at the height of fears of a Napoleonic invasion. They are the last surviving example in Jersey and are protected by the National Trust for Jersey.

Le Moulin de Lecq

Le Moulin de Lecq was one of the ancient watermills of Jersey and retains the name it bore 600 years ago. Formerly a fuller's mill and dating back to the twelfth century in parts, it is an historic landmark featuring the largest waterwheel on the island. With a diameter of 21 feet and weighing 18 tons, the outside wheel works entirely by the weight of water as it did hundreds of years ago. The two contrasting views show the mill in the 1960s, when tourism on the island was at its peak, and in June 2012, when the staff are dressed a little less colourfully.

Le Moulin de Lecq

Two views inside Le Moulin de Lecq. The top one dates from the 1960s when tourism demanded colourful traditional costumes to be worn for the visitors, whereas in 2012 this is no longer the case. The photographs do highlight, however, the magnitude and complexity of the inside waterwheel and its associated mechanism, all constructed in wood.

Grève de Lecq Bay

Today this is a very popular watering place with cafés, restaurants and hotels catering for visitors, as captured in the lower photograph, taken at the height of the holiday season in August 2011. It is a far cry from the top picture, which was probably taken in the late 1930s when there were fewer cars about and the bay had yet to be exploited commercially for tourism.

Vinchelez Lane, St Ouen

The top postcard of Vinchelez Lane by Louis Levy dates from the early 1900s and highlights the pedestrian entrance to Vinchelez de Bas. Two armorial stones above this entrance show the lozenges of de Carteret and the scallops of Dumaresq and are dated 1730 (*inset*). The same scene was captured in July 2010 and shows very little difference, except for the motor car.

Pontins Holiday Camp, Plemont

The top postcard shows Parkins Holiday Camp at Plemont on Jersey's north-west coast in the early 1960s. The Jersey Jubilee Holiday Camp was the first to occupy the site in the 1920s. This camp closed in 1939 on the outbreak of the Second World War and was taken over by the Germans during the occupation. It reopened after the cessation of hostilities and was subsequently purchased by Fred Pontin in 1961 for £375,000. It was a full-board camp, which went through a major rebuild, as shown in the bottom photograph and inset, taken in 1988.

Pontins Holiday Camp, Plemont
Two more photographs of the Pontins Holiday Camp at Plemont, taken in 1988. The camp eventually closed at the end of the 2000 season, and the site is now derelict and abandoned awaiting a decision on its future development.

Plemont Hotel

Known as the Steen Plemont Hotel, it stood on the lawn on the west side of the holiday camp and was used as a hostel and store for the camp. It caught fire during the night of 20 February 1948 and burned down, as shown in the top picture (courtesy of the Denis Holmes Collection). It was an extremely cold night with snow falling and freezing temperatures, so much so that the water that was being pumped from the holiday camp's swimming pool by the fire brigade froze solid in the line of hoses, leaving the uncontrolled fire to completely gut the building. The hotel was not rebuilt, but a café, shown in the lower 2010 photograph, now provides refreshments for visitors to Plemont Beach.

Plemont Bay

Plemont Bay is a paradise beach, with swimming, surf, sand, sunbathing and even a waterfall. As shown in the two photographs – one taken in the early 1900s, the other in August 2010 – access down to the beach is via a series of walkways and bridges, but once there it is well worth the climb.

Needle Rock, Plemont Bay
Needle Rock has been a tourist attraction at Plemont since Victorian and Edwardian times.

Caves, Plemont Bay

The caves at Plemont have always been a tourist attraction, and at one time guides would actually tout for their services and carry visitors on their backs to access the interior of the caves. Such an event is captured in the top photograph taken in the early 1900s. Today, the guides are redundant – modern visitors have no qualms about getting their feet wet and just wade in to see inside the caves.

WATERFALL CAVE, PLEMONT, JERSEY   15

Waterfall, Plemont Bay
The waterfall at Plemont then (early 1900s)
and now (August 2010).

Grosnez Castle and German MP3 Observation Tower, Les Landes

On the cliffs at Les Landes, at the most north-westerly point of Jersey, are the ruins of Grosnez Castle. Little is known about the history of this roughly built fort other than that it was erected between 1328 and 1330 as a refuge from the French. Eventually captured in 1468, by 1540 it lay in ruins. As shown in the top photograph of 2010 and the inset sketch by Jamie Leigh O'Neill, all that remains today is a gatehouse and section of wall protected by a big ditch. Contrast these ancient remains with the photograph taken in the same year of the well-preserved German MP3 observation tower, just a little further south along Les Landes.

Battery Moltke, Les Landes

At the end of the German occupation, German artillery was unceremoniously dumped into the sea from the cliffs at Les Landes. The historical significance of this ordinance has since been realised and efforts have subsequently been made by the Channel Island Occupation Society to recover such artefacts. The top photograph shows a rather rusty gun barrel being recovered from its sea grave off Les Landes in June 1992. This gun barrel has now been restored and is on display with other recovered items of artillery at Battery Moltke situated above L'Etacq Point at the southern end of Les Landes.

L'Etacquerel

Two views of L'Etacquerel, located at the northernmost end of St Ouen's Bay, at the end of Five Mile Beach. The top photograph is of pre-1939 vintage, while the lower more recent view of the same scene was taken in June 2012.

The Lobster Pot Restaurant, L'Etacquerel
Once a popular dining out spot for both islanders and visitors, the hitherto famous Lobster Pot restaurant at L'Etacquerel, shown in 1988 in the top picture, has closed its doors and by 2010, when the bottom photograph was taken, had been converted to private accommodation.

L'Etacq Tower

The construction of L'Etacq Tower on a small rocky promontory at the extreme northern end of St Ouen's Bay was started in 1832. The completed tower is shown in the pre-1939 postcard. During the occupation, this strategic point was too valuable to the Germans and they demolished L'Etacq Tower in 1942 in order to build a fortification of their own. The German bunker was a key part of Strongpoint Etacquerel. Today, as seen in the 2010 photograph, the bunker is now home to seawater tanks and cold storage for a local fish merchant.

Methodist Church, St Ouen

The oldest purpose-built Methodist church in Jersey was erected at St Ouen in 1809 and celebrated its bicentenary in 2009. By 1871, the congregation had outgrown the original church and a new, temple-like church was built next door. This new church, which could seat over 800 people, became known as the 'Cathedral of the West'. In comparing the two pictures, it seems it has changed very little between 1871 and today's photograph. Sadly however, the congregation has now dwindled and returned to the original church for services.

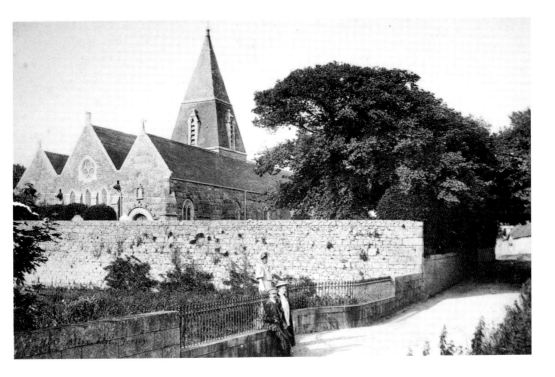

Parish Church, St Ouen

The patron saint of Normandy, St Ouen, founded a religious centre here shortly before the Viking invasions of the island. The church is also mentioned in a document signed by William before he conquered England, so part of the church building possibly predates 1066. The two views of the church date from the early 1900s and 2010 respectively, while the inset highlights the armorial bearings of the de Carteret family, members of which would have attended the church for over 800 years.

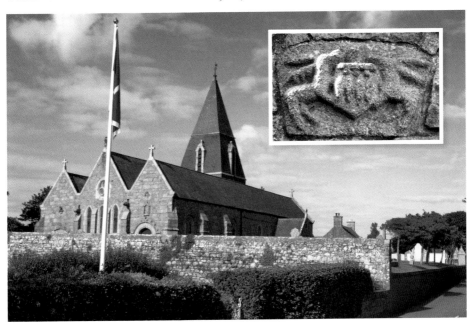

St Ouen's Manor

St Ouen, one of the twelve parishes of Jersey, is by far the largest in surface area and reputed to be the most traditional. St Ouen's Manor has been the seat of the de Carteret family for over 800 centuries and is the senior fief in the island. The earliest record of the house dates from 1135. The manor, which is still the private home of the de Carterets, is a very impressive citadel, on occasion opened to the public. The top early postcard shows the manor in the early 1900s, while the lower photograph was taken during an open day in June 1992, and the inset, provided by Barbara Wilding, was taken in November 1966.

St Ouen's Manor Gatehouse
The entrance to St Ouen's
Manor is via a very impressive
gatehouse with the driveway
leading off at a tangent from
the main A10 road, La Grande
Route de St Ouen. The bottom
photograph, taken in June 1992,
shows visitors to the island,
sisters Jacqueline and Malvina,
pointing out to the photographer
the de Carteret coat of arms
above the entrance arch.

Cabbages or Jersey Long Jacks

Once a favourite souvenir for visitors to purchase from Jersey, the cabbage or Long Jack walking sticks are now only commercially grown by one couple, Philip and Jacqueline Johnson (*inset*). Fields of giant cabbages were grown all over the island a century ago, as shown in the early 1900s postcard view. Now the cabbages are only grown in the Johnson's back garden, as captured by the camera man in August 2011. Jersey kale, or cow cabbage, has a stalk that can grow up to 18 feet in height. The leaves would be stripped off for animal fodder as the plants grew, eventually leaving the stalk bare to be dried out and turned into a practical walking stick.

Parish Church, St Peter

Two views of St Peter's church, one taken in the early 1900s, the second in August 2010 with the church now bereft of the overbearing trees. St Peter is the only parish on the island with two coastlines, those of St Ouen's Bay and St Aubin's Bay, and a large proportion of its surface area is occupied by Jersey Airport.

Jersey Airport

Jersey Airport was officially opened by Lady Coutanche on 10 March 1937. The pre-1939 top postcard shows a four-engined de Haviland DH86 Express on the tarmac in front of the original 'wedding cake' terminal and control building. In contrast, the lower postcard view shows the terminal building with the control tower on top probably in the 1970s. Jersey Airport celebrated its 75th anniversary in 2012.

Jersey Airport

Two photographs that record important changes to air traffic control at Jersey Airport. By July 2012 when the top photograph was taken, the new control tower at the airport had been completed and brought on line in 2010. The old control tower on top of the 'wedding cake' terminal building is shown under wraps while it is being dismantled. In the lower photograph, by September of the same year the terminal building is almost back to its original 1937 size.

New Air Traffic Control Tower, Jersey Airport
The top pictures on this page and the next are a split of a panoramic photograph illustrating the overall all-round view of Jersey Airport from the new air traffic control tower. The panoramic view was taken from the new control room before the new tower was finally commissioned in 2010. The bottom picture, which gives a good view of Jersey Airport from the air, was probably taken pre-1939.

New Air Traffic Control Tower, Jersey Airport
The top picture is the other half of the view from the control room that is on the preceding page, while the bottom photograph, taken in August 2010, shows the relationship of the new air traffic control tower to the other structures at Jersey Airport.

What Jersey Does Best – Seafood!
Victoria and Claire in Victoria's Fish Stall on Victoria Pier, displaying two fine lobsters caught in Jersey waters.

Acknowledgements

Compilation of this book would not have been possible without all the help and support that I have received from the following organisations and individuals, for which I offer my most sincere and grateful thanks:

Richard Blampied and staff of Aurum Manufacturing Jewellers; Richard Smale, Paul Winch and staff of the Old Court House Hotel, Gorey; Anna Baghiani of the Société Jersiaise; Liz, Dolly, Lyndon and Sam of the Pallot Steam, Motor & General Museum; Chief Fire Officer Mark James and Crew Manager Jason Betts of Jersey Fire & Rescue Service; Chief Officer Mike Bowron QPM, Insp. James Wileman, PC Chris Ingham and SOJP Welfare Adviser Mark Lamerton as well as many other members of the States of Jersey Police; Jackie Gully of Jersey Tourism; Lorenzo Nardone of the *Jersey Evening Post*; Carrie Cooper of BBC Radio Jersey; photographers Alexis Militis and Lauren Richards; caricature artist Edward Blampied; the collections of the late Denis Holmes and the late George A. Rogers; individuals Michelle Cudlipp, Maria Gouveia, Karen Hardie, Cheryl Holmes-De La Haye, Georgie Mabbs, Jamie Leigh O'Neill, Valerie Pinel, Jacqueline Bate and Gaynor and Gerald Davis.

Please accept my apologies if I have inadvertently missed anyone out of the above list.

Keith E. Morgan